Michelangelo
The Sistine Ceiling Restored

By Marcia Hall

RIZZOLI ART SERIES

Series Editor: Norma Broude

Michelangelo
(1475–1564)

The Sistine Ceiling Restored (1508–1512)

THE cleaning and conservation of Michelangelo's Sistine Chapel frescoes has transformed a familiar cultural icon and stirred up a great deal of feeling, both favoring the "new" Michelangelo and rejecting him. The papal chapel, between the Vatican palace and St. Peter's basilica, is where the conclave of cardinals meets to elect a new pope. It is one of the most visited tourist sites in the world and one of the most frequently reproduced in postcards and books. Because it holds such a prominent place in our cultural heritage, people have an almost proprietary expectation of how it should look. There are those critics of the cleaning who claim that Michelangelo was a master of chiaroscuro and that the chapel presented to us today is a stripped, sanitized, modernized version, made in the image of our own taste. Certainly the paintings that have emerged from the cleaning are a lot closer to our taste than those to be seen there before. Equally certain is that the idea of Michelangelo as the master of chiaroscuro was more to the taste of previous generations, who believed that bright color was vulgar and that serious statements could only be made in somber tones. For them, the high seriousness of Michelangelo's subject called for the suppression of color and for visual communication to be made predominantly by means of drawing. Indeed, the debate over the relative importance of *disegno* versus *colore* in painting has been going on since the sixteenth century.

For those raised in the nineteenth-century ethos, the brilliant colors we now see trivialize the message; they are appropriate to a parade or a circus, but not to the reenactment of God's Creation and redemption of humankind.[1] The explosion of color in twentieth-century art and its hard-won acceptance has not fully dislodged this prejudice, and while we may now accept as both beautiful *and* serious the joyful palette of Matisse (most of his contemporaries did not), some still expect an intellectual sobriety from the great masters of the past. The Technicolor, Kodachrome world in which we live has transformed attitudes toward color, but this is a recent development—the first big box-office Technicolor movies were made in 1939, and Kodachrome film was first marketed in 1938. We all recognize that we are the captives of contemporary taste and that it is impossible to be wholly objective. Yet there is ample evidence to assure us that the Sistine Chapel as we see it today is far closer to what Michelangelo saw when he climbed down from his scaffolding for the last time in October 1512, than it was in 1980, before the cleaning campaign was initiated.

The decision to clean the vault was made in the late 1970s by the Vatican authorities, when it was discovered that a relatively new cleaning agent, AB 57, could remove not only grime but also glue, which had proved impervious in previous cleanings. A test revealed color of a brilliance quite unanticipated. The cleaning took almost three times as long as the execution of the paintings. The chapel was built by Pope Sixtus IV, uncle of Pope Julius II, and frescoed between 1480 and 1482 by a cadre of painters, including Botticelli, Perugino, and Michelangelo's own master, Ghirlandaio. On the walls were depicted the stories of Moses and Christ, and above, in the window zone, representations of early sainted popes. There was a traditional blue vault studded with gold stars. Pope Sixtus appropriately considered the decoration of his chapel complete. However, in 1504 the shifting foundations caused a serious crack to open in the ceiling.[2] Structural work was undertaken in the hope of preventing further damage (it did not). The idea of frescoing the vault was apparently considered only when it came time to repair the damage, and Pope Julius recognized that he might embellish his uncle's chapel in a significant and fashionable way. Michelangelo was called away from the grand sculptural project of the pope's tomb, on which he had been working energetically for two years, and assigned the task of painting the ceiling. Through the confluence of artist's and pope's visionary imaginations, a scheme evolved—of a scale and scope unprecedented in Renaissance art—embodying so satisfactorily their Christian humanist values that this ceiling has come to exemplify Michelangelo and the Renaissance for us.

It had not occurred to Renaissance patrons to decorate ceilings in any but the most rudimentary ways until, toward the end of the fifteenth century, a model from classical times presented itself in the form of the newly discovered Golden House (Domus Aurea) of Nero. Beginning probably in about 1480, mysterious holes opening up on the top of the Esquiline hill in Rome began to attract attention.[3] In the second century A.D. the emperor Trajan had closed Nero's great golden palace, which had been constructed a half century earlier, sealing in, he thought forever, the evidence of Neronian decadence. Thus the palace was filled with rubble to provide foundations for the baths Trajan built atop it, a gift to the people to make amends, as it were, for Nero's effrontery and delusions of grandeur. By the last quarter of the fifteenth century the rubble had settled beneath the ruins of these baths and in places caved in, allowing glimpses of the vaults of Nero's sumptuously decorated rooms. Adventurers, including many of the leading painters, lowered themselves into these holes, equipped with candles and a box lunch, Renaissance style, and crawled in the dark on all fours to explore the passages before them. What they beheld, of course, were the vault decorations because most of the walls were still concealed by rubble. Not only did the Renaissance painters crib the style of the vault decorations they saw there—creating the style of ornament we call grotesque, from the grottoes or caves where they found them—they and their patrons, with Pope Julius in the forefront, also got the idea of decorating the vaults of their palaces and chapels with something more elaborate and imaginative than gilded stars in a blue sky.[4]

A sketch of Michelangelo's first plan for the Sistine vault (fig. 1) shows compartments separated by architectural frames imitated from the Domus Aurea, especially the Golden Vault,

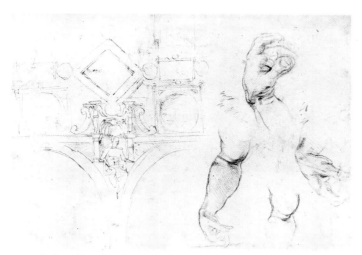

1. Michelangelo's sketch for the decoration of the vault showing the first scheme with Apostles and ornamental compartments. The British Museum, London

or Volta Dorata. As Michelangelo described it years later in one of his letters, the chapel was to have shown the twelve Apostles and grotesque ornaments. The idea of executing the far more ambitious project, telling the story of the Creation, Michelangelo credited in retrospect to himself. As the artist recounted it, he had told Pope Julius that the ceiling, as he had been ordered to do it, would be "a poor thing."[5] The reality may have differed from Michelangelo's account, but, by the time he reported it, the pope was long dead and there were few to dispute with the artist. Whatever the circumstances of the change it is obvious that the theologians of the Vatican had a hand in designing the scheme.

As designed, the vault retained the compartments of the Domus Aurea model (plate 2). Large and small panels alternate down the spine of the vault, connected at each of the corners by nudes who hold bronze shields and oak garlands with enormous acorns, the emblem of the della Rovere, the family of Sixtus IV and Julius II. In place of the enthroned Apostles of the original design are the Seers, in niches created in the fictive stone of the framework (plates 1 and 14). In the triangles (plate 13) between them that make the transition to the side walls are dark tunnels with seated figures of the same race as those who inhabit the large lunettes above the windows at the top of the chapel walls (plate 12). Originally this scheme, like that of the fifteenth-century frescoes, wrapped around the whole chapel, including the altar wall. When Michelangelo was called back years later to paint the *Last Judgment* above the altar, he had to destroy all the altar wall paintings, including two of his own lunettes.

Dovetailed into the preexisting program, Michelangelo's paintings divide into three zones (fig. 2): running down the spine are the scenes from Genesis of the Creation and the story of Noah; enthroned in niches at the sides are the Seers—the Hebrew Prophets, and their counterparts from the world of antiquity, the female Sibyls—alternating down and across the vault; in the triangles and lunettes are the forty generations of Ancestors of Christ, who link up with the New Testament life of Christ and his Apostles, depicted in the original fresco cycle. Thus the Bible story is told, from the Creation through the Fall of Man and his punishment in the Flood; the Chosen People led into the Promised Land by Moses; the history of the Hebrews and the contemporary history of the antique pagan world, referred to by the Seers, the continuity of the Old and New Testaments through the tree

of Jesse connecting David and Christ; Christ's earthly mission and the continuation of his work in the papacy.

The corner spandrels complete the program with four Old Testament scenes of salvation. Those on the entrance wall, *Judith and Her Maid* (plate 11) and *David and Goliath*, show enemies of the Hebrews, both of whom are decapitated, demonstrating the brutal treatment meted out to those who oppose God's chosen people. On the altar wall, the reference is to human redemption in Christ. In one corner, Haman is executed, not, as the Bible relates, by hanging, but by crucifixion; in the other is a representation of the Serpent of Bronze, a story commonly taken as an antetype of Christ. These two scenes, together with that at the center of the prophet Jonah, who spent three days in the belly of the whale, just as Christ would spend three days in the tomb before his resurrection, prefigure Christ's Crucifixion, Burial, and Resurrection.[6]

One of the results of the recent cleaning is that a great deal about Michelangelo's technique has been discovered. Despite his disclaimer that painting was not his profession, he was a highly skilled practitioner of the classic fresco technique, and he was not experimental. This is in sharp contrast to his older contemporary Leonardo da Vinci, who, because his artistic style was ill-suited to fresco, was driven to disastrous experimentation. Leonardo's *Last Supper*, painted in about 1495, was already showing serious signs of deterioration twenty years later,[7] and today it has virtually disappeared; most of what we can see is later retouching. Leonardo had attempted to invent a substitute for fresco—probably an oil mural technique—so that he could work at his own pace. The fresco painter must prepare the composition in detail, making careful drawings that can be transferred to the damp plaster at the moment it is ready for painting, then work surely and swiftly before the plaster dries. If a mistake is made or the painter works too slowly, the dried plaster must be laboriously removed with a chisel, or overpainted in the much less durable *secco* technique, meaning on dry plaster. Leonardo was infamous for his slow and erratic work habits. The monk who watched him working on his *Last Supper* reported with astonishment that on some days the painter would mount his scaffolding, contemplate the painting for hours, take a brush and make a few strokes, then retire,[8] a relaxed regimen not possible with fresco. Leonardo also disliked the fresco palette. Fresco is watercolor on a white wall, which means that its colors are light and bright, whereas Leonardo preferred dark and shadowy tones. He liked to blend his contours, sometimes almost losing them in smoky shadows. Michelangelo's style and work habits, by contrast, were perfectly suited to fresco. He worked with speed and with great assurance and made use of the hard-edged nature of the medium. He exploited the high contrast and brilliant color of the fresco palette to give sculpturesque clarity to his forms.

Michelangelo's use of color also differed from that of Raphael, who was working next door in the Vatican Palace on the Stanza della Segnatura at precisely the time Michelangelo was painting in the Sistine. Rather than using Michelangelo's strident contrasts, Raphael strove for mellifluous effect by juxtaposing smaller fields of color and avoiding abrupt junctures of forms. Borrowing from Leonardo, Raphael blended adjacent areas, softening the edges and thereby harmonizing them.[9]

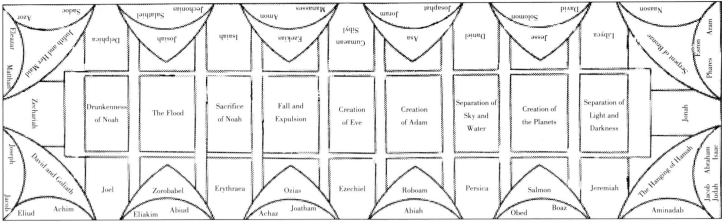

2. Diagram of the vault

Michelangelo had learned fresco technique in Florence from Domenico Ghirlandaio, who was its most accomplished practitioner in the late fifteenth century. It was Ghirlandaio who had revived the traditional methods of true fresco and abandoned the experiments, like those that Leonardo would stubbornly continue into the next century with his ill-fated *Battle of Anghiari* in the Palazzo Vecchio, in which the paint ran down the wall.

Michelangelo began to paint at the entrance to the chapel with the Noah triad of episodes and worked his way backward in biblical chronology toward the altar wall. The first Genesis scene executed, as the cleaning has confirmed, was that of *The Flood* (plate 4). Here he showed the whole panoply of humankind struggling for survival. Among those seeking the high ground at the left are a mother sheltering her children, a man carrying a woman on his back, and others who have chosen instead to laden themselves with their possessions. On the boat and the ark are those who help others from the rising water to scramble aboard, as well as those who attack them with ax or cudgel. Some stare helplessly, ignoring even a crying child, others extend themselves solicitously. Ugly self-absorption and materialism have brought God's judgment down upon them all. This crowded scene, with figures ranged across foreground, middle-ground, and background was not repeated, as Michelangelo recognized apparently that it was almost illegible from the floor, more than sixty feet away. Hereafter he arranged a small number of figures in the foreground, relief-like, against a rudimentary scenic backdrop, enlarging them to monumental proportion and giving them sculptural definition. In *The Drunkenness of Noah* (plate 3) and *The Sacrifice of Noah* (plate 5) he allows no figure to be so reduced in scale as the figures on the ark.

To be sure, he had a problem in *The Flood,* the first scene that he painted, when the plaster failed to dry properly and began to mold. According to Giorgio Vasari, who claimed that he heard it from the artist, Giuliano da Sangallo was called in to consult, and Sangallo advised Michelangelo to decrease the proportion of lime in his plaster so that it would dry more quickly. Thereafter, Michelangelo had no further trouble.[10] However the plaster must have been weakened because almost three centuries later, when there was an explosion of gunpowder stored in the Castel Sant' Angelo, about a mile away, the only part of the vault to show any damage was this area; the loss is visible in the upper right corner of *The Flood*.

Vasari also tells us that Michelangelo hired a group of assistants from Florence who were experienced in fresco, but that at a certain point he became disgusted with their work, locked them out of the chapel, and continued his work alone. The conservators have found evidence of other hands at work in *The Flood*, but after that the painting appears to be by the single hand of the master, though he certainly had assistants to prepare the paints, to lay in the day's plaster, and to do the many other menial tasks, such as lettering.

Even with only minimal assistance he worked fast: the entire cycle was completed between the spring of 1508 and end of October 1512, with six months' interval, between July or August 1510 and February 1511, when Pope Julius was away fighting his wars and the money for the painting project had run out.

The Fall of Adam and Eve and *The Expulsion from the Garden of Eden* (plate 6) Michelangelo treated as two parts of the same composition, making the point that the punishment was the inevitable consequence of the sin. They are hinged together by the serpent on the tree, who rotates 180 degrees to become the avenging angel. In a rare moment of coloristic ornament in Michelangelo's Genesis scenes, the serpent displays an appealing rainbow of tones to complement her feminine shape. Contrary to the convention, Michelangelo's Adam participates in the sin: he does not accept the apple offered by Eve, as is usually represented, but reaches for it himself with masculine aggression. Whereas Adam and Eve in Eden are beautiful and graceful, after their disgrace their figures and faces are transformed. Not only are they agonized, their faces twisted with grief, they have become ugly, undignified, and clumsy—*graceless,* in both the theological and the aesthetic sense.

For the Genesis cycle Michelangelo had few models on which to draw. Thus the images of the energized Creator have the force of novelty and invention. Never before had the Lord been shown flying through the air as we see him in *The Creation of Adam* and the other first acts of the Creation (plates 7–10); in other artists' paintings he had stood stolidly on the ground, as he does for the less inspired task of drawing Eve out of Adam's side (plate 7). Michelangelo's Adam is the perfect human form, the Renaissance re-creation of the ideal of classical antiquity. He is lacking only one thing to complete his perfection, the life-giving energy about to be passed to his languidly outstretched hand. God protects beneath his cloak a host of angels and a beautiful figure, whose hairstyle clearly marks her as a woman. She is often incorrectly identified as Eve.[11] In fact, the clue to her identity is in the biblical text of Proverbs, where God is described at the Creation as having Wisdom at his side each day. The Lord created her first, long before the earth itself, she says: "I was with him forming all things: and was delighted every day, playing before him at all times; . . . and my delights were to be with the children of men."[12] The Lord embraces Wisdom with his left arm, and the current of energy moves from her through the Lord and down his outstretched arm and hand. What is transmitted to Adam then, with the animating force, is wisdom—the quality that distinguishes man from all other creatures. There could be no more humanist image than this at the center of Michelangelo's ceiling, celebrating God's gift of wisdom to humankind.

The Creation of Adam appears to be the first Genesis scene painted after the enforced break of half a year. The painter made certain changes in the second half of the ceiling, some of which seem to have resulted from the opportunity to view from the floor what had been done, which was possible for the first time when the scaffolding was down. Michelangelo decided, for example, to enlarge the Seers in the outer bands, lowering their inscriptions to make room for the extended figures. A curious change is the omission of the consoles on either side of the inscription tablets in the Ancestor lunettes. Other changes are more gradual and seem as if they grew out of his maturing

3. *Zechariah*. Fresco, Sistine Chapel, Vatican City. Photo Vatican Museums. The prophet on the entrance wall is the first figure Michelangelo painted on the ceiling.

and expanding vision. The figures become more monumental and more awesome as we approach the altar, following the painter's progress. The paired nudes who hold the bronze shields become more energized, as well as larger, finally overlapping the scenes they frame and intruding into their spaces. Comparison of the two end-wall prophets, opposite one another at the extreme ends of the cycle, summarizes Michel-angelo's stylistic journey. Zechariah (fig. 3) on the entrance wall sits turned in profile, absorbed in his reading, noble and dignified and perfectly contained within his niche. Jonah (see plate 2), above the altar, flanked by his whale, is neither dignified nor self-contained. Caught in a moment of ecstatic vision, his feet barely touching the ground, his body thrown back, he turns his head upward in response to his vision of the Lord. Whereas the horizontals and verticals of niche and throne provide the formal grid within which Zechariah is contained, Jonah explodes out of his containing framework with vehement diagonals and oblique thrusts.

Other changes seem to have been motivated by the painter's wish for speed, for the second half of the program was executed more rapidly, and we know of reports of the pope's impatience. Michelangelo changed the way he transferred his drawings to the wall. The traditional method, which he had been using in the first campaign, involved pouncing, that is, pricking the outlines of the cartoon and squeezing charcoal through these holes. When the cartoon was removed, a dotted outline remained to guide the painting, which in places can still be seen from close up, though not, of course, from the floor. While portions of *The Creation of Adam* were transferred with pouncing, the head of Adam was incised, that is, the outline was traced into the damp plaster using a blunt instrument such as the end of a brush—a quicker method which Michelangelo continued to employ in the second campaign. Sometimes the figures overlap their outlines, as does Adam's head, having been enlarged in the course of painting. When he reached the last bay the painter apparently abandoned his cartoons altogether and painted freehand *The Separation of Light and Darkness* (plate 10), for there are no signs of either pouncing or incision. To represent this first act of the Creation, before any matter yet existed, Michelangelo invented a deliberately ethereal, unformed shape for the image of the Lord.[13]

Michelangelo made very few mistakes that he had to correct. On rare occasions he decided to make a change, such as broadening slightly a figure, perhaps to adapt it better to the curved shape of the vault. This he would sometimes do before the plaster was fully dried, perhaps at the end of the day. In such a case he could use a technique that has been called half-fresco (*mezzo-fresco*) whereby he would simply rewet the plaster with lime water and repaint. The bonding was not as complete as that of true fresco, but was considerably stronger than that formed when the change is made on already dry plaster. *Secco* was recognized in Michelangelo's time to be far less durable than fresco and was to be avoided. Michelangelo prepared his designs so carefully and was so sure-handed, we are told by the conservators, that he made only a handful of changes in *secco*.

His technique accounts for the excellent condition of his frescoes today. The principal damages have been caused by rainwater seepage and by intermittent attempts over the centuries to clean and freshen the images with glue. This glue behaved in very much the same way as varnish does on easel paintings. When it was first applied it resaturated the color and made the figures brighter and more legible. However, as time passed it attracted dirt and grime, primarily from the candles and oil lamps burned in the chapel, and darkened. It became necessary to reapply the glue, then even reinforce the darks to restore lost contrast by repainting them, and little by little the frescoes became the masterpieces of chiaroscuro that we saw until the recent cleaning.

It can be demonstrated that the frescoes darkened very quickly. A repair had to be made to *The Sacrifice of Noah* (plate 5) in the 1570s. The painter, whose name was Carnevali, proceeded very respectfully, making a tracing of the portion to be replaced before he removed the damaged plaster. He incised the outlines of his drawing of the torsos of the two figures standing at the left, then repainted, matching the colors. Just how much the colors had already darkened

4. *Isaiah.* Fresco, Sistine Chapel, Vatican City.
Photo Vatican Museums

over about a half century can be seen by the seam between Michelangelo's original color and Carnevali's "match."[14]

Despite the difference in coloring between the Sistine and other frescoes, Michelangelo used the traditional pigments, essentially the same as those employed by Raphael or Ghirlandaio. Why then do his colors today appear so much more brilliant? He was a master at achieving these effects. He used larger fields of color than anyone else, and he juxtaposed them to maximize their effect. The technique of *cangiantismo*, shifting from one hue to another in a modeling sequence, had been used by Giotto in the early fourteenth century and by many painters since. Cennino Cennini, in his "how-to" manual of Renaissance practice, describes the practice and recommends it for variety and ornamental effect. There were, after all, fewer than two dozen pigments available—Michelangelo used fourteen including black and white—so variety was creatively concocted.[15] Michelangelo used *cangianti* draperies more frequently than any painter in fresco or panel, either past or contemporary. And he used the shifts for contrast, rather than for small harmonious effects or as a bridge from one color passage to another, as did Raphael or Perugino or Pinturicchio. Then too, the sheer size of the fields being painted assured that the effect would be overwhelming.

The three zones of the ceiling—Genesis scenes, Seers, Ancestors of Christ—correspond to three levels of spiritual enlightenment, or knowledge of God, which Michelangelo expressed in the energy that each was given and in the way they were colored. The actors in the Genesis scenes are very close to God; they have intimate and firsthand knowledge of him. They are represented as full of energy and grace, fully in control of their bodies and minds. The coloring is conservative and traditional: there is very little *cangiantismo*, and what there is, is contained in small fields, such as Raphael and other painters used. For the image of God, a single-toned, deep reddish-purple mantle *(morellone)* was invented. It swirls about him, giving form to him as the essence of energy.

The Seers are more contemplative, more engrossed in their books or their prophetic visions (plates 1 and 14). Isaiah has been interrupted in his reading and turns his head with eyes closed, struggling to bring the revelation into

focus (fig. 4). They are normally colored with five hues, but where they are more active, as is the figure of Ezechiel, only three hues are used. *Cangianti* appear in the Seers with more frequency and with more prominence. It is as though color is being used to compensate for a lower level of activity: where there is a maximum of movement, the color is restrained, but where the actors are less dynamic the color redresses the balance by becoming more active. Jonah, however, all but breaks this rule. The last to be executed, his figure has a spiritual and physical energy expressed not only by the pose but by the boldly contrasted green and purple *cangianti* of his drapery.

In the lethargic and often comatose Ancestors (plates 12 and 13) the *cangianti* are concentrated: large fields of highly contrasted color lend attraction and aesthetic interest to people who are, on the whole, neither beautiful nor dynamic. Unconscious of the link they form between Abraham and Christ, they have no hint of the divine revelations that animate the Seers and fill them with seething energy. Unlike the other inhabitants of the ceiling, they live out their lives absorbed in material concerns: they cook, they sew, they dry their hair, they do the household budget. Their sole function is procreation, to pass the seed from one generation to the next, so that their lives are dominated by children who demand care and attention, sometimes overwhelming their parents, sometimes exhausting them. In Michelangelo's portrayals, they express very little emotion, but what they are allowed is restricted to a narrow range of all too human concerns—not uplifting feelings, such as joy, but rather detachment, resignation, suspicion, anxiety, hostility. They are isolated from one another and uncommunicative. Huddled in their voluminous draperies, their hands are often concealed or drop listlessly, expressing a lack of energy. These draperies are unbroken even by the large folds that we see in the more energized figures of the other two zones. The enormous fields of color that result are juxtaposed to dazzling effect. What these figures lack in animation they gain in scintillating chromaticity. Appropriate to their role in the hierarchy, however, their raiment is wholly external to them, and unnoticed by them. The impression one has is not so much that they have attired themselves vainly and gaudily in this worldly apparel as that they have been clothed in it without their knowledge, as a symbol of their unconscious role in the drama of redemption.

From the formal point of view the lunettes frame the vault. The *morellone* tone that was selected for the background of the lunettes softens the abrupt transition from side walls to vault, and it is echoed in the paler tones of it used for God's mantle in the Creation scenes. Taken together, the outer zones of the Ancestors and the Seers set up a visual excitement that complements the conservative coloring of the center. Stimulated by their aggressive color, the viewer seeks repose in the balanced and harmonious Genesis scenes. We can appreciate the carefully wrought composition if we imagine what would have happened if Michelangelo had reversed the scheme, putting the traditional coloring on the Ancestors and filling the Genesis scenes with scintillating *cangianti*.

There is a discernible logic to the new color of the Sistine frescoes, which is revealed to us because we now appreciate—and have learned even to prefer—brilliant color. It makes apparent the meaning of the cycle, both in terms of its iconography and its form. If we turn now to intellectual history, we will find another insight into the meaning of the coloring. What of the objection that the color, as we see it today, is inappropriate to the sublime subject of the frecoes? Underlying it is a moralizing interpretation of Christian theology centered on the Fall of Man that scholars in the nineteenth century believed was prevailing at the time Michelangelo was painting. This is another instance of projecting onto a past culture one's own views, for moralistic Victorians projected broadly their own judgmental views. In the past few decades we have learned much about the humanism of the papal court, especially at the time of Julius II.[16] Alerted by our own theological preferences, we have discovered that a prominent theme in Renaissance theology—as in ours today—is the celebration of the goodness of God and his Creation, rather than the proclamation of the sinfulness of man. Examined with this in mind, the story told by Michelangelo's frescoes is a story with a happy ending. The pendular swing of history from Creation, to the Fall and punishment, to rescue and the Covenant, ends not with the Flood, but with the coming of Christ and the continuance of his rule in the popes.

The fresco cycle of Michelangelo seen as the master of chiaroscuro presented a dark and ominous vision; the frescoes of the "new" Michelangelo are joyous and celebratory, in keeping with the spirit of the Renaissance and the sense of hope and possibility that, for a brief and beautiful moment, flourished then in Rome. The cleaning has given us a fresh and surprising Michelangelo, and, in the light of what we can now see, a cycle of frescoes that we can interpret as a supreme expression of the optimistic view of mankind's place in the Creation.

NOTES

1. Objections to the cleaning were recorded in the press beginning in 1987. Alexander Eliot wrote eloquently in the March–April issue of *Harvard Magazine* of that year, "The Sistine Cleanup: Agony or Ecstasy?"; vol. 89, no. 4, pp. 28–38. James Beck took the position that Michelangelo applied the glue himself as a base for modifications, corrections, and adjustments and that this "final layer" was being removed by the conservators: "The Final Layer: 'L'ultima mano' on Michelangelo's Sistine Ceiling," *Art Bulletin* 70 (1988) pp. 502–503; most recently: "Michelangelo's Pentimento Bared," *Artibus et Historiae* 24 (1991), pp. 53–63. A well-informed appraisal of the conservation and the objections that were being raised was offered by M. Kirby Talley, Jr., "Michelangelo Rediscovered," *Art News* 86, no. 6 (Summer 1987), pp. 159–170.
2. John Shearman, "The Chapel of Sixtus IV," in *The Sistine Chapel. The Art, the History, and the Restoration* (New York: Harmony Books, 1986), p. 32, based on the diaries of the Masters of Ceremonies. The first discussion with Michelangelo of the project to decorate the vault apparently took place in 1506.
3. Nicole Dacos, *La Découverte de la Domus Aurea et la formation des grotesques à la Renaissance* (London: Oxford University Press, 1969); and Juergen Schulz, "Pinturicchio and the Revival of Antiquity," *Journal of the Warburg and Courtauld Institutes* 25 (1962). On the influence of the Domus Aurea on Michelangelo's ceiling, see Herbert von Einem, *Michelangelo* [Stuttgart, 1959] (London: Methuen, 1973).
4. The vaults of chapels were frequently decorated with the four Evangelists, who fitted nicely into the quadripartite form. Pope Julius commissioned the ceiling in S. Maria del Popolo of Pinturicchio, who had previously frescoed the vault and walls of the Piccolomini Library in Siena, and the ceiling of the Stanza della Segnatura, where Raphael created compartments deriving from the new style.
5. Letter to Giovanni Francesco Fantucci written at the end of December, 1523. Charles de Tolnay, *Michelangelo: The Sistine Ceiling* (Princeton, N.J.: Princeton University Press, 1945), no. 90, p. 248.
6. On this point I prefer the interpretation in Howard Hibbard, *Michelangelo, Painter, Sculptor, Architect* (New York: Harper & Row, 1985). Three major interpretations of the iconography of the ceiling have been advanced in this century: Charles de Tolnay's neoplatonic reading given in the book cited in note 5; Frederick Hartt's Franciscan interpretation: "Lignum Vitae in Medio Paradisi: The Stanza d'Eliodoro and the Sistine Ceiling," *Art Bulletin* 32 (1950), pp. 115–145, 181–218; and most recently in Esther Gordon Dotson, "An Augustinian Interpretation of Michelangelo's Sistine Ceiling," *Art Bulletin* 61 (1979), pp. 223–256, 405–429.
7. Already in 1517 a certain Antonio de Beatis remarked that the work was deteriorating; cited in Kenneth Clark, *Leonardo da Vinci* [1939] (New York: Viking Penguin, 1989), p. 146. Quoting Clark: "Vasari, who saw it in May 1556, describes it as 'so badly handled that there is nothing visible except a muddle of blots.'"
8. The monk was Matteo Bandello; his description can be read in Clark's translation, p. 146.

9. For further discussion of the color of Leonardo, Raphael, and Michelangelo, see Marcia Hall, *Color and Meaning: Practice and Theory in Renaissance Painting* (New York: Cambridge University Press, 1992).
10. Giorgio Vasari, *The Lives of the Painters, Sculptors and Architects* [1568]. English translation: (London–New York: Everyman's Library, 1963), vol. 4, p. 125.
11. For a recent, if partial, summary of the literature, see Leo Steinberg, "Who's Who in Michelangelo's Creation of Adam: A Chronology of the Picture's Reluctant Self-Revelation," *Art Bulletin* 74 (1992), pp. 552–566, and this author's response in *Art Bulletin* 75 (1993), Letters to the Editor, June.
12. Proverbs 8:22–31, Douay translation.
13. The most complete report to date on the conservation is by the curator in charge of the project, Fabrizio Mancinelli, "Michelangelo's Frescoes in the Sistine Chapel," in *The Art of the Conservator*, ed. Andrew Oddy (London: British Museum Press, 1992), pp. 89–107. See also his article, "Michelangelo at Work: The Painting of the Ceiling," and the report of the chief restorer, Gianluigi Colalucci, on the cleaning of the lunettes: "Michelangelo's Colors Rediscovered," in *The Sistine Chapel* (1986), pp. 218–265.
14. Mancinelli, in Oddy, op. cit.
15. *The Sistine Chapel* (1986). A very interesting table of Michelangelo's pigments appears on p. 223 of the Italian edition, but the text was omitted from the English edition (though the photographs were included).
16. John O'Malley, S. J., "The Theology behind Michelangelo's Ceiling," ibid., pp. 92–148.

FURTHER READING

Condivi, Ascanio. *Life of Michelangelo,* trans. by Alice Sedgwick Wohl [Rome, 1553]. Oxford: Oxford University Press, 1976.

Ettlinger, Leopold D. *The Sistine Chapel before Michelangelo.* Oxford: Oxford University Press, 1965.

Freedberg, Sydney Joseph. *Painting of the High Renaissance in Rome and Florence.* Cambridge: Harvard University Press, 1961.

Hirst, Michael. *Michelangelo and his Drawings.* New Haven: Yale University Press, 1988.

Stinger, Charles L. *The Renaissance in Rome.* Bloomington: Indiana University Press, 1985.

First published in 1993 in the United States of America by Rizzoli International Publications, Inc.
300 Park Avenue South
New York, New York 10010

Copyright ©1993 by Rizzoli International Publications, Inc.
Text copyright ©1993 by Marcia Hall

Library of Congress Cataloging-in-Publication Data

Hall, Marcia B.
    Michelangelo : The Sistine Ceiling Restored / Marcia Hall.
    p. cm. — (Rizzoli art series)
    Includes bibliographical references and index
    ISBN 0-8478-1754-7
    1. Michelangelo Buonarroti, 1475–1564—Criticism and interpretation. 2. Mural painting and decoration, Italian—Conservation and restoration—Vatican City. 3. Mural painting and decoration, Renaissance—Conservation and restoration—Vatican City. 4. Sistine Chapel (Vatican Palace, Vatican City) I. Title. II. Series.
    ND623.B9H27   1993
    759.5—dc20   93-10440
                                                         CIP

Series Editor: Norma Broude

Series designed by José Conde and Betty Lew/Rizzoli
Editor: Charles Miers; Assistant Editor: Jennifer Condon

Printed in Italy

Front cover: See colorplate 3 (detail)

Index to Colorplates

1. *The Cumaean Sibyl*. At the center of the vault, flanking *The Creation of Eve*, the ancient seer who foretold the coming of Christ and a return of the Golden Age in Virgil's *Eclogue* IV, studies her book with puzzled gaze. Her enormous shoulders and arms express her power.

2. The vault, *The Creation of Eve* to *Jonah*. In compartments made by the fictive stone framework, large and small scenes alternate down the center, connected and animated by framing nudes. Designed to be viewed serially, from various angles and vantage points, the scheme unfolds itself slowly to the patient viewer.

3. *The Drunkenness of Noah*. Noah, inventor of wine, sampled his vintage and fell asleep naked. Discovered by his three sons, two turn respectfully away as they cover their father, while Ham looks shamelessly and points, drawing down his father's curse on him and his race for his lack of respect.

4. *The Flood*. Noah in his ark, besieged by those seeking escape from the rising water, leans out a window to check the weather. To the high land, left and right, refugees, battered by the gale, climb or drop exhausted and disconsolate. An overloaded boat makes for the ark.

5. *The Sacrifice of Noah*. As in an ancient relief that surely served as model, animals are brought in for sacrifice as Noah, standing at the center, offers thanksgiving for the ark's safe arrival. Foreground figures bustle to tend the fire and the animals.

6. *The Fall and Expulsion*. The sinners eagerly reach for the fruit in the leafy shade of the garden at the left then, at the right, stumble reluctantly on to the barren earth, their grace and beauty fallen away, as the tempting serpent twists to become the expelling angel.

7. *The Creation of Eve*. Adam, in the shadow of a tree, slumbers while God, his head bumping the top of the frame, summons Eve from his rib. She responds to his gesture with hands folded in prayer as if drawn by God's gesture and intense glance.

The Creation of Adam. Reclining listlessly on earth, Adam, built and posed like an ancient river god, extends his hand toward God, who as the embodiment of energy flies in with arm extended to transmit vitality to his beautiful human creation.

8. *The Separation of the Sky and Water*. A serene God floats toward us over the waters, revealing his gentle, benevolent nature. Michelangelo's unconventional angels, wingless and nude, are protected within his swirling mantle.

9. *The Creation of the Planets*. The Old Testament Jehovah, in such a passion of activity the accompanying angels look on in wonder, reaches out and creates the moon behind him and the sun above and brings forth grass below; then, as if in orbit, sweeps past to reveal his back.

10. *The Separation of Light and Darkness*. In the first act of the Creation and the last of the Genesis scenes executed, God is seen from below, cut by the frame, his arms pushing apart the light and the dark. Before there is yet any form, God's very mantle dissolves into the darkness.

11. *Judith and Her Maid*. The beautiful Jewish widow, having entered the tent of the enemy general Holofernes and enticed him into a state of drunkenness, cuts off his head and carries the trophy back to her people, inspiring them to fight with renewed energy.

12. *Ancestors Josaphat and Joram*, lunette. At the right a mother, her eyes closed in resigned exhaustion, copes with three exuberant children, who jump on her back, hang from her breast, or demand a loving embrace. At the left a remote father is absorbed with the household accounts.

13. *Ancestor Salmon*. The mother, observed by her husband from the penumbra behind and a child who leans on her knee and places a helpful, or interfering, hand cuts a phallic slit in the garment she holds in her lap, suggesting that domesticity and procreation sum up her life.

14. *The Prophet Daniel*. Daniel copies from the enormous book, supported between his knees, his vision of the final Resurrection of the Dead, the Last Judgment. That fresco had not yet been conceived but was painted many years later on the altar wall, toward which the prophet turns.

1. *The Cumaean Sibyl.* Fresco, Sistine Chapel, Vatican City.
Photo Vatican Museums

2. View of the vault. Sistine Chapel, Vatican City.
Photographs © Nippon Television Network Corporation, Tokyo, 1991
Courtesy of the Vatican Museums, Vatican City

3. *The Drunkenness of Noah.* Fresco, Sistine Chapel, Vatican City.
Photo Vatican Museums

4. *The Flood*. Fresco, Sistine Chapel, Vatican City. Photo Vatican Museums

5. *The Sacrifice of Noah*. Fresco, Sistine Chapel, Vatican City. Photo Vatican Museums

6. *The Fall and Expulsion.* Fresco, Sistine Chapel, Vatican City.
Photo Vatican Museums

7. *The Creation of Eve* and *The Creation of Adam*. Fresco, Sistine Chapel, Vatican City. Photo Vatican Museums

8. *The Separation of Sky and Water.* Fresco, Sistine Chapel, Vatican City.
Photo Vatican Museums

9. *The Creation of the Planets.* Fresco, Sistine Chapel, Vatican City.
Photo Vatican Museums

10. *The Separation of Light and Darkness.* Fresco, Sistine Chapel, Vatican City.
Photo Vatican Museums

11. *Judith and Her Maid.* Fresco, Sistine Chapel, Vatican City.
Photo Vatican Museums

12. *Ancestors Josaphat and Joram*, lunette. Fresco, Sistine Chapel, Vatican City. Photo: Vatican Museums.

13. *Ancestor Salmon.* Fresco, Sistine Chapel, Vatican City.
Photo Vatican Museums

14. *The Prophet Daniel.* Fresco, Sistine Chapel, Vatican City.
Photo Vatican Museums